Life on Mission
God's People Finding God's Heart for the World

Pastor Tim Harlow
Parkview Christian Church

D0166802

Copyright © 2014 for *Life on Mission — God's People Finding God's Heart for the World*

Owned by Tim Harlow, Parkview Christian Church

@tlharlow | www.lifeonmission.com

Unless otherwise noted, all Scripture quotes are taken from the HOLY BIBLE,

NEW INTERNATIONAL VERSION®. Copyright 2011 by International Bible Society.

Used by permission of Zondervan Bible Publishing House. All rights reserved.

ISBN #: 978-1-4228-0301-1

TABLE OF
CONTENTS

About The Author   4

Foreword by Rick Warren   6

Acknowledgements   10

Endorsements   12

Introduction to *Life on Mission*   16

Contributors   18

Using this Workbook   19

Outline of Each Session   20

SESSIONS

SESSION ONE – OVERVIEW   22

SESSION TWO – CONNECT   38

SESSION THREE – SERVE   54

SESSION FOUR – SHARE   68

SESSION FIVE – GROW   82

SESSION SIX – PRAY   98

APPENDICES

Frequently Asked Questions   114

Small Groups: Our Purpose   116

Small Groups: Our Values   117

Small Group Roster   118

Prayer & Praise Report   119

SMALL GROUP HOSTS

Hosting an Open House   121

Small Group Hosts 101 (Top Ten Ideas for New Hosts) 122

ABOUT THE AUTHOR

Tim Harlow, author of *Life on Mission: God's People Finding God's Heart for the World,* is the senior pastor of Parkview Christian Church, a multi-site church in the southwest suburbs of Chicago with an average weekend attendance of 8,000. (In 2013, they needed 14 services to accommodate the more than 20,000 people who celebrated Christmas at Parkview!)

According to *Outreach Magazine,* Parkview was the 76th largest church in America in 2013, and has been on the "fastest growing churches" list seven of the last 10 years.

Tim and his family moved to Chicago in 1990, when Parkview was a church of 150 people in a heavily unchurched area. Now the church is an indispensable part of the community, made up of former gang leaders and business owners, ex-strippers and soccer moms alike, all excited about Jesus, and about doing ministry in the greater Chicago area and around the world. One of Tim's very favorite stats is the 5,500+ people who have been baptized at Parkview during his watch.

Tim graduated from Ozark Christian College with a degree in Biblical literature. He received a Masters in Religion from Wayland Baptist University in Texas and a Doctorate in Ministry from Northwest Graduate School in Seattle.

Tim also lists among his favorite personal achievements being kicked out of Willie Robertson's office for having a girly beard, the time that Dave Ramsey hailed him as the second most brilliant financial mind of all time (he may have been coerced), and spending Father's Day eating steak in his backyard with Brian 'Head' Welch from Korn.

In 1984, Tim somehow convinced a hot young Ozark chick to be his wife, and Denise has been his partner in life and ministry ever since, serving as Parkview's Worship Director for the past 20 years. They have three daughters, two sons-in-law, and a grandchild on the way: Rachel (Ash), Lauren (Tommy), and Becca (don't even think about it)!

FOREWORD BY
RICK WARREN

We were sitting in an open air café in Rwanda, East Africa, when Tim Harlow first told me about his passion to write this important book. For years, Tim has been a dear friend, a fellow purpose-driven minister and pastor of the influential Parkview Christian Church. Under his care, that wonderful congregation has grown to over 8,000 worshippers gathering in multiple campuses around the south suburbs of Chicago. Tim was assisting me in encouraging the over 4,000 pastors of Rwanda who've completed the first three years of training in the P.E.A.C.E. Plan, and are now transforming that nation in amazing ways. As we talked, Tim shared his heart for reawakening the church in America for the fulfillment of the Great Commission. I told him, "You write the book, and I'll write the foreword!" You are now reading the fruit of that conversation.

This book is a vital book for a critical time. In a day when many churches have lost the vision of the Great Commission and their passion for bringing people to Christ, Tim has written a clear call to all Christians and churches to rediscover God's heartbeat for the world.

God has been on a mission since the beginning of time. From Genesis to Revelation we find God's plan to build a family for eternity, bring His lost children home, reconcile us to Himself, and then send us out to share the Good News with those He sent Jesus to die for. Jesus made it very clear that the ultimate fulfillment of God's mission will happen eventually.

The only question is whether or not our generation will get to be a part of the big ending. Jesus said, "This Good News about God's kingdom WILL be preached in ALL the world, to EVERY nation, and THEN the end will come" (Luke 9:62 LB). Jesus also said, "It is not for you to know the times or dates the Father has set by His own authority. But you will receive power when the Holy Spirit comes on you; and you will be my witnesses in Jerusalem, and in all Judea and Samaria, and to the ends of the earth" (Acts 1:7-8 NIV).

The bottom line is this: If you call yourself a disciple of Jesus, you were made for a mission! God is calling you to join Him in His mission in the world. No matter what kind of background and experiences you've had, God has planned to use it to reach others for Jesus' sake. You cannot be all God intends for you to be until you accept your life mission.

All of us want our lives to count. We want our lives to have significance. But, where does significance come from? Not from status. Not from success. Not from salary. Significance comes from service! Jesus said, "If you insist on saving your life, you will lose it. Only those who throw away their lives for my sake and for the sake of the Good News will ever know what it means to really live" (Mark 8:35 LB). This book will show you how to join God in the most significant mission in history. You will never find a more fulfilling pursuit than giving your time, talent, and treasure to being on mission with God.

Now let me say a word to pastors. For the fulfillment of God's Great Commission to happen, it will require more than just restoring the New Testament message of Jesus. We must also return to the methods Jesus used and modeled for us in His ministry. Through a close study of the Gospels, we learn not only what Jesus did in His ministry, but also how He did it! In four passages of Scripture—Matthew 10, Mark 6, Luke 9, and Luke 10—Jesus gives fifteen specific instructions to the mission teams He sent out. Unfortunately today, I don't know of a single mission strategy that is based on taking these fifteen instructions seriously. We just skip over them or explain them away due to our lack of faith.

That's why—ten years ago—I believe God led me to rediscover the Jesus model of missions, and we launched The P.E.A.C.E. Plan, built on five mission activities that Jesus modeled, and fifteen specific instructions that Jesus commanded His teams to follow when He sent them out.

FOREWORD BY
RICK WARREN

The P.E.A.C.E. Plan is simply a return to doing what Jesus did, in the way He commanded that it be done! Has Jesus' method proven effective? Yes! As the Pastor of Saddleback Church, I've watched our members catch the biblical vision of living "on mission." Today 24,869 of our members have traveled to 197 nations to serve other local churches through the purpose-driven P.E.A.C.E. Plan. I've seen firsthand, how this transformed our own congregation and also how it has blessed, reawakened, and reenergized every other church that has dared to go on mission with God.

Whether you travel the world to share Jesus, or you never venture beyond the boundaries of your home country, this guidebook can help you take your first steps in faith. (Additional information and resources are also available online at www.lifeonmission.com.)

I want to encourage you to read this book slowly, with a pen ready to underline and a journal in which to take notes as God uses these pages to speak to your heart and call you to a life of significance. Gather with other friends to study it. Give it away to anyone who has yet to experience the joy of being on mission.

My father was a pastor for more than five decades, serving mostly rural and small town churches in his ministry. But leading smaller churches didn't mean he had a small mission. One of his favorite things to do was to lead mission teams to various places around the world to help churches construct their buildings. By the time his ministry ended, he had led more than 150 building projects for churches around the world. But his efforts were never really about the physical facilities. My dad was driven by the larger mission of finding the next lost person and bringing them to Jesus.

Just two days before cancer took my father's life, he was resting in bed, very weak from chemotherapy and radiation treatment. Suddenly, my frail father began to try to get out of bed.

Frustrated by his weakness, my wife, Kay, began asking him what he needed, how we could help him, and why he wanted to get out of bed. My dad replied, "Got to save one more for Jesus! I've got to reach one more for Jesus!" He repeated that phrase over and over, maybe 125 times. In the final moments of his life, my father was declaring, for one last time, the life mission that he had lived for.

That day, with tears streaming down my face, I decided to adopt that phrase, "One More For Jesus!" as my own life mission. I cannot think of any greater goal for life. May God bless you!

Rick Warren
Author, *The Purpose Driven Life & Church*
Pastor, Saddleback Church, Lake Forest, CA
PastorRickWarren on Facebook

ACKNOWLEDGEMENTS

DEDICATION

To Denise, my partner in love and mission for 30 years. In my head and my theology, I don't believe God picks the perfect "one" for us to marry. But my heart tells me that either my theology is wrong – or I just got really lucky. I can't imagine life or mission without you.

ACKNOWLEDGEMENTS

I'm so thankful for the people who helped make this book a reality. The big step was at some restaurant in Rwanda when Rick Warren said he wanted to get behind it. I'll admit, I didn't even have to pray about that one! To Josh Warren, Nadim, Kyle, and the team at Pastors.com—this is our project, and I'm so grateful to be in partnership with you. To John, thank you for your brilliant crafting. The Saddleback team is amazing—thank you Tom, Dave, Cody, Anne, and everyone for your support.

To my daughter, Rachel, my editor and re-write specialist, I would have had a nervous breakdown without you. Thank you for helping me, and for making me a grandchild.

To my family, I love you all. Thank you, Ash, for your help on the web and your support. Lauren and Tommy — for the edits and the love and the support. I'm so proud of your ministry. Becca — you are the example of this book in every way. My family lives this mission with me.

To my parents, Dan and Faye, who lived this mission first and gave it birth in me. To my in-laws, Don and Carol, who modeled it for my wife and are my biggest encouragers. To my sister Dana, and Jay — I love the way you live this.

There is a staff full of people who work with me at Parkview that I can't live without, especially Bill, my right arm, and Jenny, my left arm. Chaz, Casey, Karyn, Scott, Debbie, Ricci, Leslie, Seth, and Wayne — thank you for your support and work on this project.

To a group of Elders who have always supported me and let me make plenty of blunders leading a church on mission — but never without their wisdom and incredible guidance.

To the Lifetogether Team — Brett and Allen — this whole thing was really your idea. Thank you for making something from nothing.

I have a band of brothers who keep me together. They are my accountability partners and life partners in every way. Ben Cachiaras, Greg Nettle, and Eddie Lowen — we will walk this journey together. And my brothers-in-law — Jack and Doug — I'm so lucky to have you with me on this journey. So many others: Rick, Dave, Cal, Mike, preacher friends who keep me in this.

To my mentors — not just my dad and father-in-law — but Uncle Roy Wheeler, Ben Merold, Don Wilson, Bob Russell, Alan Ahlgrim, Dick Alexander, and others who don't want to claim me.

Parkview — my petri dish for mission. Thank you for following a very inadequate shepherd and hardly complaining when I go after the lost sheep.

This is the hardest part of the book. There are so many people who have influenced and encouraged me, and us, in this venture. Let me just thank all of you for being in my life. Let's fill heaven together.

Finally, saving the most important for last, I thank God for loving me and for blessing me beyond measure. I turn this book over to You, knowing that I've left it in the only hands that matter.

ENDORSEMENTS

This book is where ministry meets real life. Tim's writing is funny, sincere, and passionate as he teaches how to put the gospel on display and into words - no theology degree required. Ready or not, "qualified" or not, God's inviting you to be used in a huge way… I really hope you'll pick up this book and say yes.

BRIAN "HEAD" WELCH, KORN

We have a mission that really matters -- for now and for eternity. Let my friend Tim encourage and equip you for the adventure of sharing Jesus with others. His book is an outstanding guide to a life of meaning and fulfillment.

LEE STROBEL | Best-selling Author | *The Case for Christ* and *The Case for Faith*

The mission given to the church is both the most important and the most world-changing imperative in human history. *LIFE ON MISSION* helps to make it real and compelling for our day, in our world.

JOHN ORTBERG | Senior Pastor
Menlo Park Presbyterian Church, Menlo Park, CA

Tim Harlow is deeply passionate about helping people find Christ. Discover how to connect with others, live a life of selfless service, and develop intentional relationships that will have an eternal impact as you live Life on Mission.

CRAIG GROESCHEL | Senior Pastor | LifeChurch.tv
Author of *Fight, Winning the Battles that Matter Most*

Enthusiasm and passion leap off the pages of *Life on Mission*, as Tim Harlow challenges us to love the way God loves and show others the gospel for what it is: Good News. The combination of how-to with why-to, of solid biblical teaching with a generous dose of humor, keeps it real and keeps it relevant. Ready for a mission that matters? This is it.

LIZ CURTIS HIGGS | Best-selling Author | *Bad Girls of the Bible*

I'm so happy to be on mission with Tim in Chicagoland. The challenge before us is enormous, but we are committed and believe that the harvest is ripe. What we need is a way to help our people understand how they fit into the picture. *Life on Mission* is just the ticket. It brings home the reality of the situation, which is that if ordained pastors are the only ones "doing ministry," we're in real trouble! Bringing God's love to every person in Chicago, America, and our world, will depend on every Christian understanding this mission and living it out, right where they are.

WILFREDO "CHOCO" DEJESUS | Pastor | New Life Covenant, Chicago, IL
Time Magazine 2013 100 Most Influential People in the World

Being a follower of Jesus implies movement. You can't stay where you are and follow Jesus at the same time. *Life on Mission* will do more than inform you, teach you and encourage you; it will move you. I don't know about you, but that's what I need. We all too easily end up living life on accident, or life on cruise-control, but Jesus is inviting us to live life on mission and be a part of turning this world upside down.

KYLE IDLEMAN | Pastor | Southeast Christian Church, Louisville, KY
Author of *Not a Fan* and *Gods at War*

Life on Mission couldn't have come at a better time! America has become the ultimate mission field and now she needs missionaries willing to accept the challenge to reach out and point people to the Savior of the world and Redeemer of broken lives. Tim Harlow's book lays out a clear plan of action for all of us who are willing to engage in changing our culture and helping lead people to an eternal future with God. I have accepted my mission and encourage you to read this book and do the same!

ALAN ROBERTSON | Duck Commander

Tim Harlow helps us keep "the main thing, the main thing" in his powerful book and resource, *Life on Mission*. With crystal clarity Tim shows how we can discover God's mission for our life and live it out. If every follower of Jesus read this incredible book and embraced its message, our world would be profoundly impacted for God and for good.

JUD WILHITE | Senior Pastor | Central Christian Church, Las Vegas, NV
Author of *The God of Yes*

ENDORSEMENTS

Finally, a book that steps through what it truly means to be a follower of Christ and helps you flesh that out on a daily basis. Tim's paradoxical style always hits its target. His humorous writing will help you become more serious about living a *Life on Mission*.

DAVE STONE | Pastor | Southeast Christian Church, Louisville, KY

The reason *Life on Mission* is such an important book is simply because it is a reflection of Tim Harlow's own "life on mission." Tim models life on mission, has led an amazing church to live life on mission and now, with this book, leads us all to live life on mission.

GREG NETTLE | President | Stadia Global Church Planting

Tim has captured succinctly and clearly the principles of living on mission that he has lived personally, his family has practiced, and the church he serves makes happen. Those principles are the very same that each of us are invited/called to live, regardless of our vocation or location. You will be challenged, encouraged, and stretched as you read *Life on Mission*!

RICK RUSAW | Pastor | LifeBridge Christian Church, Longmont, CO

I believe this book will be transformational, because Tim Harlow is a transformational pastor who leads a transformational church. Tim issues a personal call to break out of safe-Christianity and truly live a life that marks others.

GENE APPEL | Senior Pastor | Eastside Christian Church, Anaheim, CA

Too often over time the church drifts from its original purpose. In this book, Tim challenges us to return to the basic foundational principles that are essential to re-mission our church. This is a must read from a pastor who has grown his church consistently year after year by keeping it on mission.

DON WILSON | Senior Pastor | Christ's Church of the Valley, Peoria, AZ

If you have ever felt like your Christian life lacks passion or focus, you need to read this book! If you instinctively recognize that the church today is in trouble, but want to do more than give up, get angry, or wring your hands about it, this book is for you. If you want to live closer to the heart and actions of Jesus, you will love the practical, urgent (and funny!) guidance Tim Harlow provides. If you are part of the growing number of Christ-followers who are hungry for more than business as usual when it comes to how we live and what Church looks like, *Life on Mission* is an answer, a guide-book, and a gift.

BEN CACHIARAS | Mountain Christian Church, Joppa, MD

In a time when people are running from the church, Tim Harlow is running to it with a message every Christian needs to hear and put into practice- STOP shopping and START serving! Consumerism has a stranglehold on the American Church. *Life on Mission* challenges the followers of Jesus to walk away from the spiritual shopping carts they're steering in exchange for a basin of water and a towel. It's a book that shifts our vision from what we want to what the world needs.

JON WEECE | Southland Christian Church, KY

Tim Harlow is a leader who knows how to identify a mission and then accomplish it! In his book, *Life On Mission*, Tim gives you the practical tools needed so that you can fulfill the mission God has for you by connecting, serving, sharing, growing and praying. God has a purpose for your life and *Life On Mission* will make sure you get it done!

DAVE FERGUSON | Lead Pastor | Community Christian Church, Naperville, IL

If I had a friend living apart from God, who needed to meet Jesus through his Church, who was willing to give a church only one shot – I would want him to encounter Tim Harlow and Parkview. Tim loves the mission and loves the people it's meant for.

EDDIE LOWEN | Pastor | Westside Christian Church, Springfield, IL

INTRODUCTION BY
TIM HARLOW

GREETINGS! WELCOME TO LIFE ON MISSION!

When I look back at the months it has taken to put this study together, I'm grateful to be surrounded by such a great team of people who have spoken into these lessons. They have shared their lives and their passions, and I can hardly wait to see how God is going to use all this to bring more people into the kingdom!

I've said repeatedly that our backyard is now the largest and most diverse mission field in the world. It's almost as if God said, "Well, if My people are going to slack off from going to the world, I'm going to bring the world to them!"

I can almost bet your neighborhood is multi-cultural. The people on your street may speak different languages and live different lives than you do, but they are exactly the people Jesus had in mind when He said, "Go and make disciples of all nations" (Matthew 28:19).

Now we know that "all nations" means the world – to the very ends of the earth. But I think we've forgotten that it also means the house next door, the end of the block, and around the corner.

It's time, brothers and sisters, to refocus our lives and redefine what it means to live a life on mission. We haven't been given a new mission. We've been given a chance to re-engage with the longing of God's heart – to transform lives by bringing heaven to earth today, and earth to heaven for eternity.

Take this opportunity to meet with other Christians and to encourage one another to lovingly reach out, in word and in deed, to the people around you. Ask God to help you discover what He has planned for you: a *Life on Mission*.

Glad we're doing this together!

Tim Harlow

CONTRIBUTORS

A special word of thanks to our guest pastors and teachers, and those who shared their testimonies with us in this study guide and on the website at www.lifeonmission.com. Couldn't have done it without you!

Dick Alexander **
Alan Ahlgrim
Gene Appel *
Mike Baker
Chuck Booher
Bill Brown
Nate Bush **
Ben Cachiaras
Mindy Caliguire *
Bo Chancey
Bob Cherry **
Randy Cordell
Jason Cullum
April Diaz
Glen Elliott
Reggie Epps
Jeff Faull
Randy Gariss
Bill Geiger
Dori Gorman
Denise Harlow

Jerry Harris
Rachel Harris
Robin Hart
Tom Holladay *
Alan Hirsch *
Bill Hull
Cam Huxford *
Ken Idleman
Kyle Idleman *
Cal Jernigen *
Brian Jobe
Gary Johnson
Greg Johnson
Larry Jones
Pete Kunkle
Tim Liston
Ken Long
Greg Marksberry
Charlie McMahon
Shan Moyers
Greg Nettle

Jim Putnam
Daryl Reed **
David Roberson **
Rick Rusaw *
Diane Rusaw
Dudley Rutherford
John Scott
John Seitz
Drew Sherman
Jamie Snyder **
Rick Stedman
Dave Stone
Jeff Stone **
Lee Strobel *
Jen Taylor **
Jim Tune
Jeff Vanderstelt
Jeff Vines
Jud Wilhite *
Don Wilson

* Included on the DVD teaching
** NACC 2014 Executive Committee

Thanks, also, to the friends who provided technical services and our teaching locations.

Angelo Lazzara Productions, *Chicago, IL*
Body Tech, *Mokena, IL*
Jim Melka Landscaping & Garden Center, *Mokena, IL*
Marley Church, *Mokena, IL*
Video Editing by Michael Smith

USING THIS
WORKBOOK

(STUFF TO HELP YOU HAVE A GREAT SMALL GROUP EXPERIENCE!)

1. Notice in the Table of Contents there are three sections: Sessions; Appendices; and Small Group Hosts. Familiarize yourself with the Appendices resources.

2. If you are facilitating or hosting a small group, the Small Group Host section beginning on page 121 will give you some hard-learned experiences of others that will encourage you and help you avoid many common obstacles to effective small group hosting.

3. Use this workbook as a guide, not a straightjacket. If the group responds to the lesson in an unexpected but honest way, go with that. If you think of a better question than the next one in the lesson, ask it. Take to heart the insights included in the FAQs beginning on page 114.

4. Finally, enjoy your small group experience! We believe that you can't grow spiritually unless you are connected relationally. God designed us that way. God wants to use other people to grow us, and He wants to use us to grow other people. That's because life-change happens best in community.

OUTLINE OF
EACH SESSION

Each session of this *Life on Mission* study provides a healthy balance that includes teaching, evangelism, ministry, and practical exercises. As you apply truths from each section in your discussion every week, it will be exciting to see how God works in the lives of your group members and their families.

A TYPICAL GROUP SESSION FOR LIFE ON MISSION INCLUDES:

WEEKLY MEMORY VERSES

For each session, we have provided a Memory Verse that emphasizes an important truth from the session. This is an optional exercise, but we strongly encourage you to give this habit a try because one of the best things we can do is to regularly fill our minds with God's Word.

HANGING OUT

Developing relationships with a few people who really know you and have earned your trust can help you to live the life Jesus wants you to live. The HANGING OUT section is a fun time where we can get to know each other better and get comfortable before we dive into the weekly teaching.

WATCH AND LEARN / DVD TEACHING SEGMENT

Every session combines video teaching segments from Pastor Tim Harlow, along with leadership insights and many inspiring, personal stories of men and women demonstrating real life-change.

FIGURING IT OUT

As a follow-up to the video teaching, this section includes questions designed to encourage discussion and to help you get the most out of what the leaders and speakers shared from their experiences, as well as from God's Word. The focus is not on accumulating information, but rather on applying insights practically and creatively - in the heart as well as the head. (NOTE: Questions in this section with an * indicate the best ones to use if time is short.)

LIVING IT OUT

Nothing that we learn in this study will mean a thing if we don't allow it transform our everyday lives. In James 1:22, we are told to be, "doers of the Word, not just hearers." As His disciples, Jesus wants us to help people connect with Him in a close and personal way, and to live life according to God's Word. This section provides practical ways that we can reach out to those around us, and to go beyond Bible study to biblical living.

DIGGING DEEPER

If you have time and want to dig deeper, we've provided additional Bible passages and questions. This section is useful for homework, additional group discussion, and personal study.

DAILY QUIET TIME

With each session, we provide daily Scriptures to reflect on between group meetings. We suggest you use these QUIET TIME pages to seek God on your own throughout the week. This time at home should begin and end with prayer. Don't hurry; take enough time to hear God's direction.

SESSION ONE
OVERVIEW

What does it mean to be a witness? In a courtroom, witnesses are called to tell their stories - to testify about what they have seen or experienced. Why? Just because they have interesting stories? No. It's because their stories impact others, and have the potential to change the destiny of many.

Jesus calls us as His followers to be witnesses - to tell our stories. We don't have to be experts in theology or know all the answers about the Bible. We do have to be willing to tell people why we believe, and how we have been changed by the hope that is in us.

Really, that's what it means to live life on mission. To see opportunities right in front of us: opportunities to tell our stories in a way that will change someone's destiny.

Welcome to your *Life on Mission.*

WHAT DOES IT MEAN TO BE A WITNESS?
THAT'S WHAT THIS FIRST SESSION IS ABOUT.

MEMORY VERSE

But you will receive power when the Holy Spirit comes on you; and you will be my witnesses in Jerusalem, and in all Judea and Samaria, and to the ends of the earth.

Acts 1:8

HANGING OUT

Open your group with prayer. Be willing to be real and honest. Remind the group to respect confidentiality; commit to keeping prayer requests and current needs within the group.

Over the next six weeks, we're going to start every session by praying together and just hanging out so we can get to know each other a little better.

So relax, settle in, and let's get started!

1. As we begin, what's the first thing that comes to mind when you think of the title of this study, *Life on Mission*?

2. What is the most extraordinary thing you have ever witnessed?

3. During today's video teaching, Pastor Tim is in downtown Chicago, one of the largest cities in the world. If you had to choose, are you a big city or small town person and why?

Watch the DVD teaching for this session, using this **Teaching Notes** section to fill in the blanks, and record key thoughts, questions, and statements you want to remember or look into further.

OVERVIEW

The problem is, telling people about Jesus has become such a _____!

If _____ isn't applied, it's _____.

Christians are supposed to make things _____.

A _____ relationship is the key.

TEACHING NOTES

FIGURING IT OUT

If time is short, the questions marked with an * should be given priority.

1. What comments from the DVD teaching impacted you the most?

_____

_____

_____

_____

_____

2. * Think about your life. Where has God given you influence? (For instance, your school, neighborhood, workplace, etc.) In other words, where are you already connected with other people?

_____

_____

_____

_____

_____

3. How often do you spend time with other people who aren't Christians? When you find yourself in social situations with people who don't know Jesus, do you feel:

a) comfortable and friendly

b) somewhat uncomfortable

c) anxious

d) I am rarely in social situations with non-Christians.

Now take a minute to elaborate on your choice.

4. * Think about people you know who don't follow Jesus. How would you describe them? When you think about building a friendship with them, what's your gut reaction?

    _____

    _____

    _____

    _____

5. * Lee Strobel shared Jesus' metaphor about being salt and light, and said that Jesus tells us to, "live lives that are salty, that make people thirst for God." How can the way you live your life make people thirst for God?

    _____

    _____

    _____

    _____

6. **Read Ephesians 2:8-10.** God has planned some things for you to do. What do you think they are?

    _____

    _____

    _____

    _____

    _____

LIVING IT OUT

IN THIS SECTION, TALK ABOUT HOW YOU WILL APPLY THE WISDOM YOU'VE LEARNED FROM THE TEACHING AND BIBLE STUDY. THEN THINK ABOUT PRACTICAL STEPS YOU CAN TAKE IN THE COMING WEEK TO LIVE OUT WHAT YOU'VE LEARNED.

According to Rick Warren, there are two things you can't do in heaven; you can't sin and you can't tell people about Jesus.

Which of the following most accurately describes your view on sharing your faith:

a) It makes me so nervous, I go out of my way to avoid it.

b) I'll answer questions if someone asks, but I don't bring it up.

c) I feel guilty that I don't do it more often, so occasionally I'll try.

d) I evangelize regularly and start conversations about God with strangers all the time.

For more *Life on Mission* resources, visit
www.lifeonmission.com.

Pastor Tim said we were called to be witnesses: not judges, defense attorneys, or prosecutors. Generally speaking, how can we expect people to react when they feel they're being judged and attacked versus being compassionately told good news?

_____

_____

_____

Read Acts 1:8. When you think of Pastor Tim's phone and current location analogy from the DVD teaching, who are the people in your family, neighborhood, or workplace who need some salt and light?

_____

_____

_____

Read Matthew 9:37-38. The need is obvious and immediate. How does this inspire you to live a life on mission?

_____

_____

_____

_____

CLOSE IN PRAYER

If you feel God nudging you to go deeper, take some time between now and our next meeting to dig into His Word. Explore the Bible passages related to this session's theme on your own, jotting your reflections in a journal or in this study guide. A great way to gain insight on a passage is to read it in several different translations. You may want to use a Bible app or website to compare translations.

▌DIGGING DEEPER

READ LUKE 15:11–32.

The parable of the prodigal son may be the best known of Jesus' stories. It's actually the story of three people: father, son, and older brother. Each of us might identify with any of those characters in His lesson. Each person in the story also represents a mission - a way of living with a certain purpose in mind. The main lesson, of course, is that at some point, each of us plays the role of the prodigal child who needs to come home. The underlying challenge in the parable is the question; how long does it take to develop the father's heart?

1. Verse 11 says, "Jesus continued." He's already told the parables of the lost coin and the lost sheep. How does the shift from coin to sheep to son make these three stories work together?

    _____

    _____

    _____

2. In each of these three parables, something is lost, and then found. What conclusions can we draw about people who are "lost" and how God feels about them?

    _____

    _____

    _____

3. How does this story change the way you see people who are rebelling or wandering away from God?

    _____

    _____

    _____

    _____

    _____

4. If you met the prodigal son today - a promiscuous young man who was squandering his inheritance on partying - what would you think of him? How is this different from how the father sees him?

    _____

    _____

    _____

    _____

    _____

5. In what ways do we sometimes act like the older brother in this story? In what ways could we call him a prodigal/wanderer, too?

    _____

    _____

    _____

    _____

DAILY QUIET TIME

Each day, read the daily verses and give prayerful consideration to what you learn about God, His Spirit, and His place in your life. Then record your thoughts, insights, or prayers on the lines below each verse.

DAY 1: "Don't you have a saying, 'It's still four months until harvest'? I tell you, open your eyes and look at the fields! They are ripe for harvest." (John 4:35)

What "fields" are around you? What keeps you from seeing "the harvest" (the people who need to know Jesus)?

_____

_____

_____

_____

_____

DAY 2: "In the same way, I tell you, there is rejoicing in the presence of the angels of God over one sinner who repents." (Luke 15:10)

How does it make you feel to realize that God and His angels have rejoiced over you? How will living life on mission lead to rejoicing?

_____

_____

_____

_____

_____

DAY 3: "So then, just as you received Christ Jesus as Lord, continue to live your lives in him, rooted and built up in him, strengthened in the faith as you were taught, and overflowing with thankfulness." (Colossians 2:6-7)

What practices or habits will help you to stay "rooted and built up in Him"? What is one thing in your life that would change if you were continually "overflowing with thankfulness"?

_____

_____

_____

_____

DAY 4: "But God demonstrates his own love for us in this: While we were still sinners, Christ died for us." (Romans 5:8)

How has God demonstrated to you that you are dear to Him?

_____

_____

_____

_____

DAY 5: "But you will receive power when the Holy Spirit comes on you; and you will be my witnesses in Jerusalem, and in all Judea and Samaria, and to the ends of the earth." (Acts 1:8)

In this verse, Jesus restates His commission to His disciples. To what degree would you say this is a description of your life? What needs to change?

_____

_____

_____

_____

SESSION TWO
CONNECT

t may seem obvious, but if we never connect and spend time with people who are far from God, it's going to be impossible to introduce them to Jesus. Jesus set an example for us by hanging around with people who needed Him – people who needed to be healed, not just physically but spiritually.

Jesus often did this around a meal, but He also did it as He walked around throughout His day. He didn't wait for people to come to Him - He went to them. He was always connecting with people, engaging them in conversation. He was great at listening, and He was always asking questions.

Many of us tend to keep our social and relational circles limited to people who act and believe just as we do. Or we think that connecting with people who aren't Christians means preaching at them, not just hanging out with them.

Jesus calls His followers not only to believe in Him, but to live like Him. That often begins with choosing to connect with people who are far from God.

MEMORY VERSE

"While Jesus was having dinner at Matthew's house, many tax collectors and sinners came and ate with him and his disciples. When the Pharisees saw this, they asked his disciples, "Why does your teacher eat with tax collectors and sinners?" On hearing this, Jesus said, "It is not the healthy who need a doctor, but the sick. But go and learn what this means: 'I desire mercy, not sacrifice.' For I have not come to call the righteous, but sinners."

Matthew 9:10-13

HANGING OUT

Open your group with prayer. Be willing to be real and honest. Remind the group to respect confidentiality; commit to keeping prayer requests and current needs within the group.

1. During the OVERVIEW session, Pastor Tim challenged us to be salt and light. As you went throughout your week, how were you able to **shake,** and where were you able to **shine**?

2. Today's teaching takes place in a health club, a great place to connect with people. Where's your favorite place to hang out with friends?

3. Tell about a time when you were welcomed to a gathering or meal as an newcomer. What happened and how did it make you feel?

WATCH AND LEARN

CONNECT

Watch the DVD teaching for this session, using this **Teaching Notes** section to fill in the blanks, and record key thoughts, questions, and statements you want to remember or look into further.

CONNECT

Jesus was sent on a _____.

Your mission is _____.

If the body's not moving, it's not _____.

Jesus said His mission was to _____ and _____ the lost.

When you go out to your Jerusalem to be God with meat, just be

_____.

TEACHING NOTES

FIGURING IT OUT

*If time is short, the questions marked with an * should be given priority.*

1. What was your most intense take-away from the stories and teaching we just heard? Why is it important that we hang out with people who are not followers of Jesus?

   _____

   _____

   _____

   _____

2. * What are some of your non-church activities (such as sports, work, volunteering at your child's school, etc.) where you could connect with people who aren't Christians? Since you're already in those places, what can you do to initiate relationships with others?

   _____

   _____

   _____

   _____

3. * Gene Appel talked about the importance of good questions. These are not "pickup lines" or interrogations. They are not yes/no questions. In your own life, what kinds of questions draw you into conversation?

   _____

   _____

   _____

   _____

4. *** Read Matthew 9:10-13.** Eating with someone is a way of demonstrating how much you value a person. Why was it so shocking to people when they saw who Jesus was sharing a meal with?

_____

_____

_____

_____

_____

_____

5. What barriers get in the way of you inviting your neighbors into your home for a simple meal and conversation?

_____

_____

_____

_____

_____

_____

LIVING IT OUT

IN THIS SECTION, TALK ABOUT HOW YOU WILL APPLY THE WISDOM YOU'VE LEARNED FROM THE TEACHING AND BIBLE STUDY. THEN THINK ABOUT PRACTICAL STEPS YOU CAN TAKE IN THE COMING WEEK TO LIVE OUT WHAT YOU'VE LEARNED.

Pastor Tim intentionally works out at a health club so that he can connect with people who are far from God. What places would you consider visiting in order to connect with people who need to meet Jesus?

_____

_____

_____

_____

Mindy Caliguire was intentional about having meals and snacks in her home for her son's friends who were far from God. What can you do this week to create a safe and welcoming environment in your home in order to connect with people in your life?

_____

_____

_____

_____

Pastor Tim gave us a LIVING IT OUT challenge this week. He asked, "Who is in your Jerusalem right now that you can connect with, and what are you going to do about it?"

_____

_____

_____

_____

_____

Non-Christians don't just hear our words, they watch how we live. Take some time this week to identify behaviors in your life that might be stumbling blocks that prevent others from being open to hearing about Jesus. Make a commitment to ask God to help you remove any behaviors that don't align with the faith you profess.

CLOSE IN PRAYER

For more
Life on Mission resources, visit
www.lifeonmission.com.

If you feel God nudging you to go deeper, take some time between now and our next meeting to dig into His Word. Explore the Bible passages related to this session's theme on your own, jotting your reflections in a journal or in this study guide. A great way to gain insight on a passage is to read it in several different translations. You may want to use a Bible app or website to compare translations.

▊ DIGGING DEEPER

READ MATTHEW 9:1–13.

While many of us first met Jesus in a religious setting, sooner or later we have to learn that Jesus is Lord over all of life. If He's only the Master when we're in church or with other religious people, then He's not really the Master.

This passage invites us to think about how we have followed Jesus and what we have done to bring others along.

1. If Matthew was one of the eyewitnesses of Jesus' miracle with the paralyzed man, how do you think it set him up for the invitation to follow?

   _____

   _____

   _____

2. Matthew invited all his friends over for a life-changing party. Who showed up and what did they experience?

   _____

   _____

   _____

DIGGING DEEPER

AS WE READ MATTHEW 9, it's interesting to note that Matthew invited friends who were far from God to come and have dinner with Jesus. In the ancient Middle East, sharing a meal was particularly significant. It showed acceptance and friendship on a deeper level than a shared meal in our culture does today. Jesus fellowshipped with "sinners" before they ever thought about repentance or lifestyle change. It's likely that many of them ended up believing in Him, but His acceptance of them wasn't contingent upon that. He loves sinners unconditionally, and asks us to do the same.

3. Why do you think Jesus was so "at home" with these sinners?

     _____

     _____

     _____

4. What was Jesus expecting us to do in response to His words that night: "But go and learn what this means: 'I desire mercy, not sacrifice.' For I have not come to call the righteous, but sinners" (Matthew 9:13).

     _____

     _____

     _____

5. What is one way you have "gone and learned"?

     _____

     _____

     _____

DAILY QUIET TIME

Each day, read the daily verses and give prayerful consideration to what you learn about God, His Spirit, and His place in your life. Then record your thoughts, insights, or prayers on the lines below each verse.

DAY 1: "Share with the Lord's people who are in need. Practice hospitality. Bless those who persecute you; bless and do not curse. Rejoice with those who rejoice; mourn with those who mourn. Live in harmony with one another. Do not be proud, but be willing to associate with people of low position. Do not be conceited." (Romans 12:13-16)

How much of this passage would you say reflects your lifestyle? What does this list have to do with connecting with others?

_____

_____

_____

DAY 2: "But go and learn what this means: 'I desire mercy, not sacrifice.' For I have not come to call the righteous, but sinners." (Matthew 9:13)

What have you done since the small group session to "go and learn" what Jesus said?

_____

_____

_____

DAY 3: "Keep on loving one another as brothers and sisters. Do not forget to show hospitality to strangers, for by so doing some people have shown hospitality to angels without knowing it." (Hebrews 13:1-2)

What are some ways you can "show hospitality to strangers"?

_____

_____

_____

DAY 4: "For the Son of Man came to seek and to save the lost." (Luke 19:10)

We often talk about people being spiritual "seekers," but who does this verse say is doing the seeking? What does that imply for us as His followers (those who want to live as He did)?

_____

_____

_____

_____

_____

DAY 5: "Neither do people light a lamp and put it under a bowl. Instead they put it on its stand, and it gives light to everyone in the house. In the same way, let your light shine before others, that they may see your good deeds and glorify your Father in heaven." (Matthew 5:15-16)

What does it mean to let your light shine? What is one way you can do that? How would it help you connect with others?

_____

_____

_____

_____

_____

_____

SESSION THREE
SERVE

Jesus told us to love God and love others. Love, however, is often misunderstood. (We "love" chocolate, for instance!) To simply say that we love, or even have warm feelings toward someone, is not enough. Loving others means taking action and serving them.

In fact, Jesus told us that when we serve others in practical ways – feeding them, clothing them, sheltering them, visiting them - that is how we show our love for Him. God sees our service toward others as love toward Him.

Beyond that, our service to others may introduce them to the love of God. When we serve them, we break down walls in ways that words simply cannot. We show them that they are not "projects" to us - people we're merely trying to convert. Rather, they are unique individuals who are loved by God, and one of the ways they'll believe that is if we show them His love by serving them.

WE SERVE OTHERS IN PRACTICAL WAYS.
THAT IS HOW WE SHOW OUR LOVE FOR HIM.

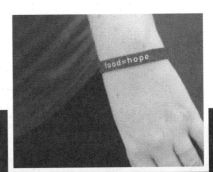

MEMORY VERSE

The King will reply, 'Truly I tell you, whatever you did for one of the least of these brothers and sisters of mine, you did for me.'

Matthew 25:40

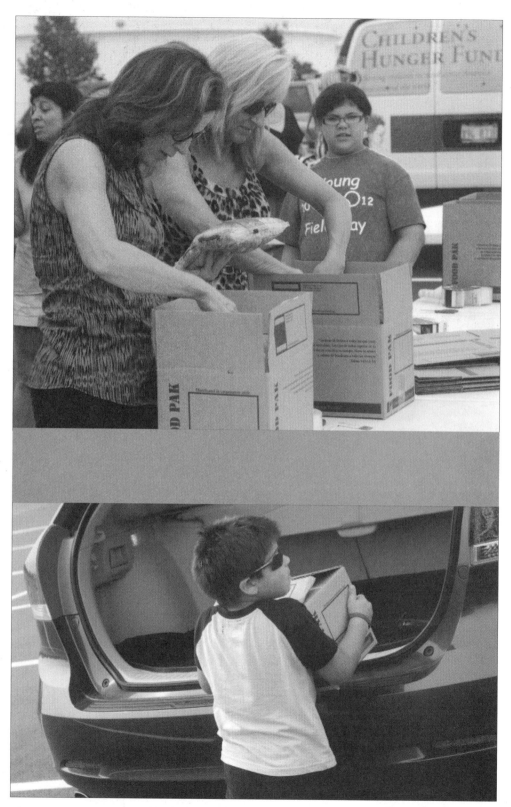

HANGING OUT

Open your group with prayer. Be willing to be real and honest. Remind the group to respect confidentiality; commit to keeping prayer requests and current needs within the group.

1. What opportunities did God give you during the last week to CONNECT with someone who is far from God?

2. Moving from one house to another can be a really stressful time in our lives: a time when we really need others to help us out. How many times have you moved in your life?

3. Share a story (funny or not so funny), about a time that you moved to a new home. Did your friends step up or did they make excuses? Did all your belongings arrive in one piece?

WATCH AND LEARN

SERVE

Watch the DVD teaching for this session,
using this **Teaching Notes** section to fill in the
blanks, and record key thoughts, questions, and statements
you want to remember or look into further.

SERVE

It's going from being a _____ to being _____.

In the backyard, they are still _____. When you start to serve them, they
come _____.

I believe the problem with modern Christianity is that the world sees
us as _____ way more than they see us as _____.

2 mission busters: _____ and _____

I honestly believe that the greatest _____ to the mission of
Jesus is the _____ of His agents.

TEACHING NOTES

FIGURING IT OUT

If time is short, the questions marked with an * should be given priority.

1. Most of us hate interruptions, but it is often life's interruptions that provide us with opportunities to serve others. How do you typically respond to interruptions or inconveniences?

    _____

    _____

    _____

    _____

2. **Read Luke 10:30-32.** The Priest and Levite are supposed to be the ones living life on mission for God. Has there been a time in your life when you let the comfort and convenience of your daily routine stop you from meeting a need?

    _____

    _____

    _____

    _____

3. * **Read Luke 10:33-37.** The Good Samaritan was inconvenienced and had to go out of his way to help the man in the story. Has there been a time when you were willing to step out of your comfort zone to meet a pressing need?

    _____

    _____

    _____

    _____

FIGURING IT OUT

4. What are some ways that you've experienced God's love and kindness through the acts of another person?

_____

_____

_____

_____

5. * What are some needs that you've noticed lately - opportunities where you could possibly serve others? How did you respond to those needs?

_____

_____

_____

_____

6. * In order to introduce people to Jesus, we have to genuinely love them - we need to make them not just friends but family. What steps are you taking (or do you want to take) to love people in this way?

_____

_____

_____

_____

LIVING IT OUT

IN THIS SECTION, TALK ABOUT HOW YOU WILL APPLY THE WISDOM YOU'VE LEARNED FROM THE TEACHING AND BIBLE STUDY. THEN THINK ABOUT PRACTICAL STEPS YOU CAN TAKE IN THE COMING WEEK TO LIVE OUT WHAT YOU'VE LEARNED.

Read Philippians 2:5. Our goal is to look like Jesus. What does that mean to you?

_____

_____

_____

_____

Read Matthew 25:40, our memory verse. Share with the group any people in your life (co-workers, family, friends, neighbors, etc.) who are far from God and have immediate needs that aren't being met.

_____

_____

_____

_____

What are some skills or resources that God has given you that can be used to meet these needs (e.g., cooking, providing transportation, mowing the lawn, etc.)? If you are not able to meet the needs yourself, do you know someone who could?

_____

_____

_____

We can often find significant opportunities to discover, practice, and improve our capacity to serve in Christ's name in our own home. In what ways are you serving those who live with you under the same roof?

_____

_____

_____

Over the coming week, consider inviting a friend to attend our group or a weekend worship service, and possibly enjoy a meal together afterward.

CLOSE IN PRAYER

For more *Life on Mission* resources, visit www.lifeonmission.com.

If you feel God nudging you to go deeper, take some time between now and our next meeting to dig into His Word. Explore the Bible passages related to this session's theme on your own, jotting your reflections in a journal or in this study guide. A great way to gain insight on a passage is to read it in several different translations. You may want to use a Bible app or website to compare translations.

▌ DIGGING DEEPER

READ JOHN 13:1-17

The final meal Jesus shared with His disciples was unforgettable. It's mentioned in all four Gospels, and gets an extended description in John 13–17. Jesus not only taught about the significance of love in everything we do and say, but He demonstrated and highlighted the truth of His words. He definitely practiced what He preached!

1. What did Jesus say with His actions in these verses? What was the main point of His words?

     _____

     _____

2. Why do you think Jesus was presented with the opportunity to wash the disciples' feet?

     _____

     _____

3. How did Jesus connect the reality of our relationship with Him to the realities of our relationships with one another?

     _____

     _____

4. In what way does Peter's response in verses 6–10 parallel how many of us respond to sacrificial service?

     _____

     _____

DAILY QUIET TIME

Each day, read the daily verses and give prayerful consideration to what you learn about God, His Spirit, and His place in your life. Then record your thoughts, insights, or prayers on the lines below each verse.

DAY 1: "Instead, whoever wants to become great among you must be your servant, and whoever wants to be first must be your slave—just as the Son of Man did not come to be served, but to serve, and to give his life as a ransom for many" (Matthew 20:26-28).

Spend some time praying and asking God to show you how He wants you to live out this verse in your life. Specifically, who is He asking you to serve?

_____

_____

_____

_____

_____

DAY 2: "The most important one," answered Jesus, "is this: 'Hear, O Israel: The Lord our God, the Lord is one. Love the Lord your God with all your heart and with all your soul and with all your mind and with all your strength.' The second is this: 'Love your neighbor as yourself.' There is no commandment greater than these'" (Mark 12:29-31).

How would someone know by examining your life that this two-part commandment is the driving force in your life?

_____

_____

_____

_____

_____

DAY 3: "Therefore, I urge you, brothers and sisters, in view of God's mercy, to offer your bodies as a living sacrifice, holy and pleasing to God - this is your true and proper worship (Romans 12:1)

How is serving others a way of "offering your body" to God?

_____

_____

_____

_____

DAY 4: "Give fair judgment to the poor and the orphan; uphold the rights of the oppressed and the destitute. Rescue the poor and helpless; deliver them from the grasp of evil people" (Psalm 82:3-4).

God calls us to not only serve those who can return the favor, but to serve people who are poor and oppressed. How often do you interact with "the oppressed and the destitute"? How is your life insulated from people in this situation?

_____

_____

_____

_____

DAY 5: "A new command I give you: Love one another. As I have loved you, so you must love one another. By this everyone will know that you are my disciples, if you love one another." (John 13:34-35)

As you participate in this small group, what opportunities are you finding to love and serve others?

_____

_____

_____

_____

SESSION FOUR
SHARE

In this session, we want to talk about being ready for the inevitable "Why are you doing this?" question that will come up when we are genuinely interested in other people. Even if we are reaching out in imperfect ways, the impact of authentic love is so counter to the normal experiences of most people that they are intrigued. So they may open the door with a question.

On the other hand, it may be that people appreciate our kindness, but never ask why we do what we do. They may just assume that we're "nice." So at some point, God asks us to be bold, and to initiate the conversation. This can be a bit scary. We certainly don't want to alienate people or push them away from God! And truth be told, we don't want them to think we're strange. But because Jesus is the way, the truth, the life, and the only way to the Father, then we need to help people understand that.

We can share the Gospel in a relevant way when we simply tell our own story. We don't have to be Bible experts or have answers to all of the hard theological questions. We just need to be ready to share our own experiences, and to state clearly and simply how Jesus has changed our lives.

MEMORY VERSE

But in your hearts revere Christ as Lord. Always be prepared to give an answer to everyone who asks you to give the reason for the hope that you have. But do this with gentleness and respect.

1 Peter 3:15

HANGING OUT

Open your group with prayer. Be willing to be real and honest. Remind the group to respect confidentiality; commit to keeping prayer requests and current needs within the group.

1. What opportunity or opportunities did God give you to SERVE others this last week?

2. Who is the first person you call or text when you want to share good news? Why?

3. What's the weirdest thing someone has shared with you lately?

WATCH AND LEARN

SHARE

Watch the DVD teaching for this session, using this **Teaching Notes** section to fill in the blanks, and record key thoughts, questions, and statements you want to remember or look into further.

SHARE

Because at some point - _____ HAVE TO BE A PART OF THE MISSION.

Always be _____ to give an answer to everyone who asks you to give the reason for the _____ that you have. 1 Peter 3:15

You have a story: a _____ story.

What's the best way to get into telling your story? One way is to _____ for _____ that Jesus has helped you with.

You can also just sort of relate to a _____ _____.

Friends don't keep _____ _____ from other friends.

TEACHING NOTES

FIGURING IT OUT

*If time is short, the questions marked with an * should be given priority.*

1. Who explained the Good News about Jesus to you? How did they do it? What was your initial response?

    _____

    _____

    _____

    _____

    _____

2. What do you think keeps people from talking about Jesus or sharing the Gospel?

    _____

    _____

    _____

    _____

3. * Our memory verse for this session is 1 Peter 3:15. "But in your hearts revere Christ as Lord. Always be prepared to give an answer to everyone who asks you to give the reason for the hope that you have. But do this with gentleness and respect."

    Are you living a life that motivates people to ask about the hope that is in you?

    _____

    _____

    _____

    _____

FIGURING IT OUT

4. Have you ever been asked to give a reason for the hope people see in you?

    _____

    _____

    _____

5. *** Read John 9:25.** When the blind man was asked a question that he didn't know how to answer, he simply said, "I don't know." How does it relieve your fears to hear that "I don't know" is an acceptable way to answer a question about God?

    _____

    _____

    _____

    _____

6. * Colossians 4:5-6 says, "Be wise in the way you act toward outsiders; make the most of every opportunity. Let your conversation be always full of grace, seasoned with salt, so that you may know how to answer everyone."

    In order for your conversation to be full of grace, you must be able to listen. How will listening well empower you to share the Gospel more effectively?

    _____

    _____

    _____

    _____

    _____

LIVING IT OUT

IN THIS SECTION, TALK ABOUT HOW YOU WILL APPLY THE WISDOM YOU'VE LEARNED FROM THE TEACHING AND BIBLE STUDY. THEN THINK ABOUT PRACTICAL STEPS YOU CAN TAKE IN THE COMING WEEK TO LIVE OUT WHAT YOU'VE LEARNED.

Each of us is automatically an expert on our own story, and on our own experiences. But most people aren't necessarily ready to hear the "epic" version of our stories.

What do you think are the most important parts of your story. Include your life before you came to know Jesus, and also how you've changed since He came into your life.

_____

_____

_____

_____

_____

_____

_____

For more
Life on Mission resources, visit
www.lifeonmission.com.

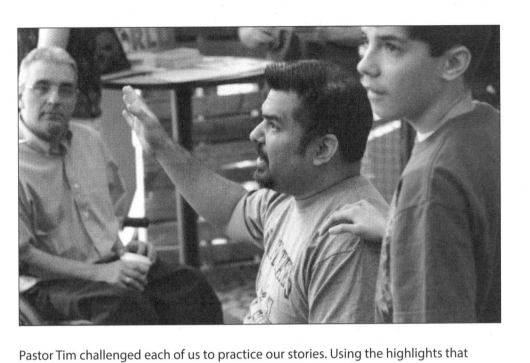

Pastor Tim challenged each of us to practice our stories. Using the highlights that we identified in the previous question, let's take turns practicing our stories in under two minutes.

_____

_____

_____

_____

_____

Who is one person in your life who seems to be curious about spiritual matters? Spend a little time praying for that person, and for the opportunity to share the two minute version of your story sometime in the near future.

_____

_____

CLOSE IN PRAYER

If you feel God nudging you to go deeper, take some time between now and our next meeting to dig into His Word. Explore the Bible passages related to this session's theme on your own, jotting your reflections in a journal or in this study guide. A great way to gain insight on a passage is to read it in several different translations. You may want to use a Bible app or website to compare translations.

▌DIGGING DEEPER

READ ACTS 25:23—26:32

The account of Paul's appearance before King Agrippa provides a great example of how to give an account of God's work in your life. You may never get the chance to speak to a president or influential leader, but you can trust God to give you a chance to tell your story to many people along the way. If He opens the door, are you willing to tell your story?

1. How much of Paul's story was BC (before Christ) and how much AC (after Christ)?

   _____

   _____

2. In what ways did both Festus and Agrippa demonstrate possible responses to your story?

   _____

   _____

3. Why is it important, as in this case, to realize that you may not ever find out the results of telling your own story?

   _____

   _____

4. As you think about Paul's setting and his story, what other conclusions do you draw that affect your view of God's prompting in your life?

   _____

   _____

DAILY QUIET TIME

Each day, read the daily verses and give prayerful consideration to what you learn about God, His Spirit, and His place in your life. Then record your thoughts, insights, or prayers on the lines below each verse.

DAY 1: "And without faith it is impossible to please God, because anyone who comes to him must believe that he exists and that he rewards those who earnestly seek him." (Hebrews 11:6)

What does it mean to seek God, and how should that affect our willingness to share with fellow travelers in life?

_____

_____

_____

_____

_____

DAY 2: "But God demonstrates his own love for us in this: While we were still sinners, Christ died for us." (Romans 5:8)

How can you incorporate this verse into your story? Try writing out your faith story (Before Christ, Meeting Christ, After Christ) and put this verse into your narrative.

_____

_____

_____

_____

_____

_____

DAY 3: "Salvation is found in no one else, for there is no other name under heaven given to mankind by which we must be saved" (Acts 4:12).

Can you think of two or three friends or acquaintances who don't know this truth? How could you begin to share with them? Spend some time praying about that.

_____

_____

_____

_____

DAY 4: ""Listen and I'll tell you what God has done for me" (Psalm 66:16, NCV).

Based on your story, what would you say to someone if he or she wanted what you have in Christ? What has God done for you?

_____

_____

_____

_____

DAY 5: "But in your hearts revere Christ as Lord. Always be prepared to give an answer to everyone who asks you to give the reason for the hope that you have. But do this with gentleness and respect... (1 Peter 3:15).

What specific words would you use to convey "gentleness and respect" when you share your story? What words would you avoid? (What Christian jargon can you weed out of your faith story?)

_____

_____

_____

_____

_____

SESSION FIVE
GROW

Have you ever noticed a change for the better in another person? Did you wonder what happened to bring about that change? Having a relationship with Jesus should change us. The Bible tells us that we are to be transformed. In Galatians 5:22-23, we are reminded that having the Holy Spirit within us should bring about positive character change.

The most compelling evidence for the power of God to change a life is simply that: a changed life. When you change and grow into someone who is more like Jesus - someone who is more loving, patient, and kind than ever before - people notice. It's not a matter of focusing on self-improvement and trying to change ourselves. It's about inviting God in, turning it all over to Him, and asking Him to do the heavy lifting.

So this week, we're going to talk about growth. We are called to be disciples of Jesus and that means that we are to develop daily habits that help us to be more like Him as we continually rely on Him, and learn from His example. And we are also called to make disciples, and to help them do the same!

THE MOST COMPELLING EVIDENCE FOR THE POWER OF
GOD TO CHANGE A LIFE IS SIMPLY THAT: *A CHANGED LIFE*

MEMORY VERSE

Do not conform to the pattern
of this world, but be transformed
by the renewing of your mind.
Then you will be able to test and
approve what God's will is—His
good, pleasing and perfect will.

Romans 12:2

HANGING OUT

Open your group with prayer. Be willing to be real and honest. Remind the group to respect confidentiality; commit to keeping prayer requests and current needs within the group.

1. What was one idea that you took away from last week's SHARE discussion? Did God give you an opportunity to share your two minute story with anyone during the past week?

2. This week as we turn to GROW, let's talk foliage! What was the reason behind the last time you sent or received flowers?

3. Do you have a green thumb? Share with the group any gardening successes (or failures) you have experienced.

WATCH AND LEARN

GROW

Watch the DVD teaching for this session,
using this **Teaching Notes** section to fill in the
blanks, and record key thoughts, questions, and statements
you want to remember or look into further.

GROW

Matthew 28 doesn't say, "Go and make _____."

This is about a _____ of _____.

_____ and _____ are not two
different things we do. It's all a part of a process.

When we are the _____ of Christ, then we can serve the
_____ of Christ.

It's not until you grow that you can _____ _____.

Learning can happen in the _____, but spiritual growth has to
happen in _____.

TEACHING NOTES

FIGURING IT OUT

*If time is short, the questions marked with an * should be given priority.*

1. Has there been a spiritual mentor in your life? If so, how has that helped you to grow?

_____

_____

_____

_____

2. * Kyle Idleman talked about the words of Jesus in John 15, where He compared branches (us) to being connected to the vine (Himself). Kyle offered, "A simple challenge to Christians; be the branch." What do you think that means? How can you "be the branch"?

_____

_____

_____

_____

_____

3. As you are out there making disciples, you (as a disciple yourself) get a chance to grow through those relationships. Describe a time that you grew as a result of helping someone else understand Jesus better.

_____

_____

_____

_____

FIGURING IT OUT

4. * What spiritual disciplines or practices help to connect you with the Holy Spirit and train you for godliness? How does that help you "put the Gospel on display" for others.

_____

_____

_____

_____

_____

_____

5. * Pastor Tim challenged us to make disciples, not converts. He noted that evangelism and discipleship are not two different things we do, but that each of them are part of one process: that of making disciples. What happens when people separate evangelism and discipleship?

_____

_____

_____

_____

_____

_____

_____

LIVING IT OUT

IN THIS SECTION, TALK ABOUT HOW YOU WILL APPLY THE WISDOM YOU'VE
LEARNED FROM THE TEACHING AND BIBLE STUDY. THEN THINK ABOUT PRACTICAL
STEPS YOU CAN TAKE IN THE COMING WEEK TO LIVE OUT WHAT YOU'VE LEARNED.

Read Galatians 5:22-23. From the list of the fruits of the Spirit, identify the one that
you wish was true in your life. What are you going to do this week to grow in the area
you identified?

_____

_____

_____

_____

As you grow in this area, how will this empower you to help others grow?

_____

_____

_____

_____

In her testimony, Katherine talked about discipling people in her life. She said, "You really only need to be one step ahead of them." What does that mean to you?

_____

_____

_____

_____

Who in your life are you one step ahead of, and currently discipling? If you are having a difficult time coming up with a name, commit to praying and watching for an opportunity to help someone grow as a Christ-follower.

_____

_____

CLOSE IN PRAYER

For more *Life on Mission* resources, visit www.lifeonmission.com.

If you feel God nudging you to go deeper, take some time between now and our next meeting to dig into His Word. Explore the Bible passages related to this session's theme on your own, jotting your reflections in a journal or in this study guide. A great way to gain insight on a passage is to read it in several different translations. You may want to use a Bible app or website to compare translations.

⁝ DIGGING DEEPER

READ HEBREWS 10:24-25

"And let us consider how we may spur one another on toward love and good deeds, not giving up meeting together, as some are in the habit of doing, but encouraging one another—and all the more as you see the Day approaching."

1. What do these verses tell us about the role of community in our spiritual growth?

    _____

    _____

    _____

2. The words "one another" appear twice here, and countless times throughout the New Testament. Use a Bible app or online version to find other references to "one another." What does this tell us about how we are to walk with Jesus?

    _____

    _____

    _____

3. Who spurs you on to love and good deeds? If you don't have someone in your life who does that, pray about finding someone you can encourage, and who will also be an encouragement to you.

    _____

    _____

    _____

DAILY QUIET TIME

Each day, read the daily verses and give prayerful consideration to what you learn about God, His Spirit, and His place in your life. Then record your thoughts, insights, or prayers on the lines below each verse.

DAY 1: "Being confident of this, that he who began a good work in you will carry it on to completion until the day of Christ Jesus." (Philippians 1:6)

Growth is affected by how we respond to what God wants to do in our lives. How are you responding to God's good work in you?

_____

_____

_____

_____

DAY 2: "Therefore, since we are surrounded by such a great cloud of witnesses, let us throw off everything that hinders and the sin that so easily entangles. And let us run with perseverance the race marked out for us, fixing our eyes on Jesus, the pioneer and perfecter of faith. For the joy set before him he endured the cross, scorning its shame, and sat down at the right hand of the throne of God.." (Hebrews 12:1-2)

What are three things in your life that need to be "thrown off" so that you can run with perseverance?

_____

_____

_____

_____

_____

DAY 3: "Hear, O Israel: The Lord our God, the Lord is one. Love the Lord your God with all your heart and with all your soul and with all your strength. These commandments that I give you today are to be on your hearts. Impress them on your children. Talk about them when you sit at home and when you walk along the road, when you lie down and when you get up. Tie them as symbols on your hands and bind them on your foreheads. Write them on the doorframes of your houses and on your gates. " (Deuteronomy 6:4-9)

In what ways are loving the Lord your God a continual practice and topic of conversation in your house as you grow together?

_____

_____

_____

DAY 4: "So then, just as you received Christ Jesus as Lord, continue to live your lives in him, rooted and built up in him, strengthened in the faith as you were taught, and overflowing with thankfulness." (Colossians 2:6-7)

In what ways would you say your roots are growing down and your branches are growing up in Christ?

_____

_____

_____

DAY 5: "I am the vine; you are the branches. If you remain in me and I in you, you will bear much fruit; apart from me you can do nothing." (John 15:5)

What are you currently doing to remain connected to the vine? What fruit are you seeing as a result?

_____

_____

_____

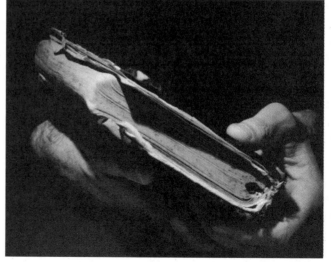

SESSION SIX
PRAY

f we are on a mission to connect, serve, share, and grow, doesn't it make sense that we should stay in communication with the One who is sending us out? The One who knows far more than we do and is able to help us accomplish that mission? Prayer is how we stay connected to God, and is the source of our power and strength.

Finding God's heart for the world starts with prayer because it moves us from our perspective to His perspective. It allows us to invite God into our concerns, needs, and desires, but it also makes us realize that our compassion and care for our neighbors is only a hint of what God feels toward them.

Without God's help, which we access through prayer, our mission will surely fail. Instead of prayer being the last thing we do after we have exhausted all other means, let's put it front and center where it belongs. Prayer is a central, consistent means to bring God's power to bear on every life we touch.

We cannot live a *life on mission* without it.

MEMORY VERSE

And pray in the Spirit on all occasions with all
kinds of prayers and requests. With this in mind, be
alert and always keep on praying for all the Lord's people.

Ephesians 6:18

HANGING OUT

Open your group with prayer. Be willing to be real and honest. Remind the group to respect confidentiality; commit to keeping prayer requests and current needs within the group.

1. What opportunity did God give you last week to help someone GROW in his or her faith?

2. Today we are going to focus on prayer. Have you ever prayed about the outcome of a sporting event? Discuss!

3. When you were growing up, how did you pray (if you prayed at all)? How has your understanding of prayer changed over the years?

WATCH AND LEARN

PRAY

Watch the DVD teaching for this session,
using this **Teaching Notes** section to fill in the
blanks, and record key thoughts, questions, and statements
you want to remember or look into further.

PRAY

I have to admit to you that ending up here is _____ and
_____ at the same time.

God does want to _____ you, it's just not _____ you.

That's what prayer is, my friends. It's our _____ point to God's
_____ _____.

You have to take the _____ to God before you take _____ to the people.

But when I take the time to _____, I see them the way God sees them – as a
lost child that the father can't wait to have _____.

TEACHING NOTES

FIGURING IT OUT

*If time is short, the questions marked with an * should be given priority.*

1. *** Read 1 Thessalonians 5:16-18.** How can you begin to make prayer a habit or automatic reaction to times of both difficulty and joy?

   _____

   _____

   _____

   _____

   _____

2. Have you ever been mad at God for not saying yes to one of your prayers, only to realize later that God's plan was far better than what you wanted?

   _____

   _____

   _____

   _____

   _____

3. Tell the group about a time someone prayed for you in a moment of need and you felt God's presence more powerfully as a result.

   _____

   _____

   _____

   _____

   _____

FIGURING IT OUT

4. **Read Ephesians 3:20.** When you pray for someone who is far from God, or for someone whose spiritual condition you really don't know, what are you expecting God to do?

   _____

   _____

   _____

   _____

5. * Do you ever find yourself drifting away from communication with God? How does that impact your ability to live a life on mission?

   _____

   _____

   _____

   _____

   _____

6. * In what ways has your prayer life been challenged by this session's teaching?

   _____

   _____

   _____

   _____

LIVING IT OUT

IN THIS SECTION, TALK ABOUT HOW YOU WILL APPLY THE WISDOM YOU'VE LEARNED FROM THE TEACHING AND BIBLE STUDY. THEN THINK ABOUT PRACTICAL STEPS YOU CAN TAKE IN THE COMING WEEK TO LIVE OUT WHAT YOU'VE LEARNED.

As followers of Jesus, we are promised the Holy Spirit. The Holy Spirit empowers us to do more than we could on our own. What are you doing today that you could not do apart from the power of God?

_____

_____

_____

_____

_____

_____

Very few people would turn down the offer to be prayed for. Who can you offer to pray for this week? (And make sure you really pray!!)

_____

_____

Read Luke 10:02. Pastor Tim asked us all to set our alarms on our phones, or on our bedside tables, to 10:02 and pray specifically for the Lord of the Harvest to send workers. **It's exciting to think about the thousands of people who have done this study, all praying together at the same time for God to send more people who will be living LIFE ON MISSION!!**

Six months from now, what do you think you will be doing differently as a result of being a part of this group?

_____

_____

_____

_____

Congratulations! You've made it through this
Life on Mission study! Maybe the next step that
God has for you is to start your own small group
and invite people who are far from God.

For more *Life on Mission* resources,
visit www.lifeonmission.com.

CLOSE IN PRAYER

STAFF

If you feel God nudging you to go deeper, take some time between now and our next meeting to dig into His Word. Explore the Bible passages related to this session's theme on your own, jotting your reflections in a journal or in this study guide. A great way to gain insight on a passage is to read it in several different translations. You may want to use a Bible app or website to compare translations.

▊DIGGING DEEPER

READ LUKE 15:1–7.

This parable reveals the heart of God to seek and save the lost. In His teaching throughout the entire chapter, Jesus confronts the judgmental attitudes that were swirling around Him. He did not take lightly the lack of concern that was being shown for those who were considered to be "tax collectors (sell-outs) and sinners."

1. How does Luke describe the setting in which Jesus told this and other parables in chapter 15? Why does the audience matter in this case?

   _____

   _____

   _____

   _____

2. How does this parable reveal the importance of being in tune, or in sync, with how God views people who are lost in the world?

   _____

   _____

   _____

   _____

3. How would you make a case for prayer from this parable?

_____

_____

_____

_____

4. As a result of prayer, when was the last time your church was able to join with the angels and celebrate the homecoming of a lost sheep? What conclusion might you draw from this?

_____

_____

_____

_____

5. In what ways are praying with others such a part of your life that people would notice if you stopped doing it?

_____

_____

_____

_____

DAILY QUIET TIME

Each day, read the daily verses and give prayerful consideration to what you learn about God, His Spirit, and His place in your life. Then record your thoughts, insights, or prayers on the lines below each verse.

DAY 1: "Very early in the morning, while it was still dark, Jesus got up, left the house and went off to a solitary place, where he prayed." (Mark 1:35)

What do you think Jesus was praying about during those regular times alone with God? What would have to happen for your priorities to be closer to His?

_____

_____

_____

_____

_____

DAY 2: "But when you pray, go into your room, close the door and pray to your Father, who is unseen. Then your Father, who sees what is done in secret, will reward you." (Matthew 6:6)

Why is it important for some of our praying to be done in secret?

_____

_____

_____

_____

_____

DAY 3: "Is anyone among you in trouble? Let them pray. Is anyone happy? Let them sing songs of praise. Is anyone among you sick? Let them call the elders of the church to pray over them and anoint them with oil in the name of the Lord." (James 5:13-14)

What is your typical response to times of trouble or happiness? What does this verse tell us it should be?

_____

_____

_____

DAY 4: "Devote yourselves to prayer, being watchful and thankful. And pray for us, too, that God may open a door for our message, so that we may proclaim the mystery of Christ, for which I am in chains. Pray that I may proclaim it clearly, as I should." (Colossians 4:2-4)

Paul encouraged prayer, and he also asked for prayer. Who prays regularly for you? Who is someone you could ask to pray for you?

_____

_____

_____

DAY 5: "Then he said to his disciples, "The harvest is plentiful but the workers are few. Ask the Lord of the harvest, therefore, to send out workers into his harvest field" (Matthew 9:37–38).

Why do you think that instead of simply telling them to go be workers, Jesus said, "Ask the Lord of the harvest…"? What does this tell us about our first priority when living life on mission?

_____

_____

_____

APPENDICES

GREAT
RESOURCES
TO HELP MAKE YOUR
SMALL GROUP
EXPERIENCE
EVEN BETTER!

FREQUENTLY ASKED
QUESTIONS

WHAT DO WE DO ON THE FIRST NIGHT OF OUR GROUP?

Like all fun things in life–have a party! A "get to know you" coffee, dinner, or dessert is a great way to launch a new study. But most importantly, have fun before your study time begins.

WHERE DO WE FIND NEW MEMBERS FOR OUR GROUP?

This can be troubling, especially for new groups that have only a few people or for existing groups that lose a few people along the way. We encourage you to pray with your group and then brainstorm a list of people from work, church, your neighborhood, your children's school, family, the gym, and so forth. Then have each group member invite several of the people on his or her list.

No matter how you find members, it's vital you stay on the lookout for new people to join your group. All groups tend to go through healthy attrition–the result of moves, releasing new leaders, ministry opportunities, and so forth–and if the group gets too small, it could be at risk of shutting down. If you and your group stay open, you'll be amazed at the people God sends your way. The next person just might become a friend for life. You never know!

HOW LONG WILL THIS GROUP MEET?

Once you come to the end of this 6-week study, it's totally up to you! Each group member may decide if he or she wants to continue on for another study, or if they want to use this as a stepping-stone into another group experience. Either way, enjoy the journey.

WHAT IS THE TIME REQUIREMENT EACH WEEK?

1.5 to 2 hours. As the Host, you might commit a little extra time between meetings each week to review the DVD and discussion questions, as well as pray for your group members.

CAN WE DO THIS STUDY ON OUR OWN?

Absolutely! This may sound crazy but one of the best ways to do this study is not with a full house but with a few friends. You may choose to gather with one other couple who would enjoy going out or having a quiet dinner and then walking through this study.

WHAT IF THIS GROUP IS NOT WORKING FOR US?

You're not alone! This could be the result of a personality conflict, life-stage difference, geographical distance, level of spiritual maturity, or any number of things. Relax.

Pray for God's direction, and at the end of this 6-week study, decide whether to continue with this group or find another. You don't buy the first car you look at or marry the first person you date, and the same goes with a group. Don't bail out before the 6 weeks are up–God might have something to teach you. Also, don't run from conflict or prejudge people before you have given them a chance. God is still working in you, too!

HOW DO WE HANDLE THE CHILD CARE NEEDS IN OUR GROUP?

Very carefully. Seriously, this can be a sensitive issue. We suggest you empower the group to openly brainstorm solutions. You may try one option that works for a while and then adjust over time. Our favorite approach is for adults to meet in the living room or dining room, and to share the cost of a babysitter (or two) who can be with the kids in a different part of the house. In this way, parents don't have to be away from their children all evening when their children are too young to be left at home. A second option is to use one home for the kids and a second home (close by or a phone call away) for the adults. A third idea is to rotate the responsibility of providing a lesson or care for the children either in the same home or in another home nearby. This can be an incredible blessing for kids.

Finally, the most common idea is to decide you need to have a night to invest in your spiritual lives individually or as a couple, and to make your own arrangements for child care. No matter what decision the group makes, the best approach is to dialogue openly about both the problem and the solution.

OUR PURPOSE

TO PROVIDE A PREDICTABLE ENVIRONMENT WHERE
PARTICIPANTS EXPERIENCE AUTHENTIC COMMUNITY AND
SPIRITUAL GROWTH.

OUR VALUES

GROUP ATTENDANCE	To give priority to the group meeting. We will call or email if we will be late or absent.
SAFE ENVIRONMENT	To help create a safe place where people can be heard and feel loved. (Please, no quick answers, snap judgments, or simple fixes.)
RESPECT DIFFERENCES	To be gentle and gracious to people with different spiritual maturity, personal opinions, temperaments, or "imperfections" in fellow group members. We are all works in progress.
CONFIDENTIALITY	To keep anything that is shared strictly confidential and within the group, and to avoid sharing improper information about those outside the group.
ENCOURAGEMENT FOR GROWTH	To be not just takers but givers of life. We want to spiritually multiply our life by serving others with our God-given gifts.
SHARED OWNERSHIP	To remember every member is a minister and to ensure each attender will share a small team role or responsibility over time.
ROTATING HOSTS AND HOMES	To encourage different people to host the group in their homes, and to rotate the responsibility of facilitating each meeting.

SMALL GROUP
ROSTER

NAME

PRAYER & PRAISE
REPORT

PRAYER & PRAISE
REPORT

HOSTING AN
OPEN HOUSE

If you're starting a new group, try planning an "open house" before your first formal group meeting. Even if you only have two to four core members, it's a great way to break the ice and to consider prayerfully who else might be open to join you over the next few weeks. You can also use this kick-off meeting to hand out study guides, spend some time getting to know each other, discuss each person's expectations for the group, and briefly pray for each other.

A simple meal or good desserts always make a kick-off meeting more fun. After people introduce themselves and share how they ended up being at the meeting (you can play a game to see who has the wildest story!), have everyone respond to a few icebreaker questions: "What is your favorite family vacation?" or "What is one thing you love about your church/our community?" or "What are three things about your life growing up that most

people here don't know?" Next, ask everyone to tell what he or she hopes to get out of the study.

Finally, set an open chair (maybe two) in the center of your group and explain it represents someone who would enjoy or benefit from this group, but who isn't here yet. Ask people to pray about whom they could invite to join the group over the next few weeks.

Don't worry about ending up with too many people; you can always have one discussion circle in the living room and another in the dining room after you watch the lesson. Each group could then report prayer requests and progress at the end of the session.

You can skip this kick-off meeting if your time is limited, but you'll experience a huge benefit if you take the time to connect with each other in this way.

HOST TRAINING 101

SIX GREAT IDEAS FOR NEW HOSTS

CONGRATULATIONS! YOU HAVE RESPONDED TO THE CALL TO HELP SHEPHERD JESUS' FLOCK. THERE ARE FEW OTHER TASKS IN THE FAMILY OF GOD THAT SURPASS THE CONTRIBUTION YOU WILL BE MAKING. AS YOU PREPARE TO HOST, HERE ARE A FEW THOUGHTS TO KEEP IN MIND.

1. Remember you are not alone. God knows everything about you, and He knew you would be asked to host your group. Remember it is common to feel you are not ready to lead. Moses, Solomon, Jeremiah, and Timothy - they all were reluctant. God promises, "Never will I leave you; never will I forsake you" (Hebrews 13:5). You will be blessed as you serve.

2. Don't try to do it alone. If you can enlist someone to help you host the group, you will find your experience to be much richer.

3. Just be yourself. If you won't be you, who will? God wants you to use your unique gifts and temperament. Don't try to do things exactly like another host; do them in a way that fits you! Just admit it when you don't have an answer, and apologize when you make a mistake. Your group will love you for it, and you'll sleep better at night!

4. Prepare for your meeting ahead of time. Review the session and write down your responses to each question. Pay special attention to the LIVING IT OUT questions that ask group members to do something other than engage in discussion.

5. Pray for your group members by name. Before you begin your session, go around the room in your mind and pray for each member by name. You may want to review the prayer list at least once a week. Ask God to use your time together to touch the heart of every person uniquely. Expect God to lead you to whomever He wants you to encourage or challenge in a special way. If you listen, God will surely lead!

6. When you ask a question, be patient. Someone will eventually respond. Sometimes people need a moment or two of silence to think about the question, and if silence doesn't bother you, it won't bother anyone else. After someone responds, affirm the response with a simple "thanks" or "good job." Then ask, "How about somebody else?" or "Would someone who hasn't shared like to add anything?" Be sensitive to new people or reluctant members who aren't ready to say, pray, or do anything. If you give them a safe setting, they will blossom over time.

NOTES

NOTES

NOTES

NOTES

NOTES